Late Crossing

Anne-Marie Fyfe

Late Crossing

Rockingham Press

Published in 1999
by
The Rockingham Press
11 Musley Lane,
Ware, Herts
SG12 7EN

Copyright © Anne-Marie Fyfe, 1999

British Library Cataloguing-in-Publication Data

A catalogue record for this book
is available from the British Library

ISBN 1 873468 63 6

Printed in Great Britain
by Biddles Limited, Guildford

Printed on Recycled Paper

for Cahal, Matthew & Ruth

Contents

I

Motel	10
Broken Journey	11
Interstate	12
Endgame	13
The Next Stop	14
On the Rue des Tournelles	15
Between Stations	16
East River Wind	17
The Fishing Hut	18
No Jitterbugging in the Aisles, Please!	19
Foreseeing Death	20
Postscript	21
Former Selves	22
Holy Trinity Church, Clapham	23
Friday	24
Home	25
RMS "Titanic"	26
No Far Shore	27

II

The Orchard	30
Midday Bus	31
Two Storeys	32
A Woman's Place	33
Backyard	34
Catching Your Death	35
The Half-Light	36
Upturn	37
Midnight Mass	38
Cushendall, 1959	39
Newsflash	40
Outboard	41
Hallstand	44

III

Story-Teller	48
Where there is Hope	49
Afternoons	50
Birds, Martinstown	51
Feet First	52
Naming	53
Leavetaking	54
Matins	55
Waking	56
Moonbeam	57
The Heart's Needle	58
Interior	59
Getting Ready	60
Morning Shuttle	61
Consultant	62
On My Birthday	63
The Quiet	64
Gift	65

IV

The Sea of Moyle	68
First Nightmare of the Holiday	69
The Heron	70
Late Crossing	71
New Year Departures	72
November	73
May	73
Last Things	74
Number Nine	75
Tennessee Waltz	76
A House by the Sea	77
Coming Back	78
Woodsmoke	79

Acknowledgments

Acknowledgements are due to the editors of the following publications in which some of these poems first appeared: *The Independent, London Magazine, Poetry Ireland Review, The Rialto, Smiths Knoll, Poetry Durham, Tears in the Fence, Poetry London Newsletter, Seam, Fire, Other Poetry, Navis, Nova Poetica, Southfield, Manifest* and *Gairfish*.

"Where There is Hope" appeared in *Riding Pillion: The Poetry Business Anthology, 1994*; "Upturn" and "Hallstand" appeared in *The Ring of Words: Poems from The Daily Telegraph Arvon International Poetry Competition, 1998*. Some of the poems appeared in the pamphlet *A House by the Sea* (Bellmead, 1995).

I

The soul has bandaged moments

Emily Dickinson

Motel

Here in this sweltered suburb
the call of an owl disquiets
and for a moment I'm that child
who believes in the banshee.
I draw the dampened sheet closer,
push my foot across to feel
for yours – but waken alone:
a woman in a late-night movie
screams through the wall; over the way
there's the faintest of opera;
and still an owl is calling –
the irrefutable wail
of a mother for a lost child.

Broken Journey

Cruising down the freeway
on an interstate long-haul
he lost his place
for a moment;
stared blankly
at an unfamiliar landscape,
a lunch-box, magazines,
a pair of hands on the wheel.

Dropping a gear instinctively
he swerved off
into a truck-stop
at the precise second
when the shutter lifted
and he was back
firmly in the picture.
He limped towards the diner
reassured by his reflection
in the plate-glass front.
He remembered his mother
unable to find the kitchen;
she had ended her days
in a family of strangers.
But he was only forty.

He ordered strong coffee
and dialled his woman;
his heart lurched and steadied
when he heard her voice.
He told her he'd be
in time for supper,
asked about the kids.
Picking up a burger
he hit the road again
nervously, looking out
for the right exit sign.

Interstate

Half-eaten fries, the remains of hash browns,
fill the table's distance between them.
She scoops the car-keys, says she'll not be long.

In the washroom mirror she checks her face
close-up; sees years of wearied waiting.
She steps into a sticky afternoon.

How long before he'll notice, before he'll ask –
the forecourt is nauseous with diesel and ocean –
ask if anyone's seen a woman in middle years.

She's onto the freeway, jittering across lanes.
And why, he'll wonder, now that the kids are gone,
now that they're free to hit the road each spring.

She overtakes on automatic, clearing Carolina –
recalls the one dream he has left, of building a boat;
upriver in summer; dry-dock in winter. The two of them.

An unforeseen calm settles with sundown: she longs
for nightfall on unbroken stretches of highway.
It's clear ahead as far as her eyes can see.

Endgame

Before dying beyond my means
I shall adorn Les Deux Magots
daily in dazzling earrings
fill spiralling *cahiers* with aged
bon mots, exchange *confidences*
with superior waiters and when
a certain set gather in Père-Lachaise
to murmur a little softly
how life fled *(aujourd'hui ou peut-être
hier?)* the *inconnu* in black
pillbox hat and veil who regrets
nothing – cryptic among epitaphs -
won't believe that no-one
gets out of here alive.

The Next Stop

In bed he turned over
and heard in the stillness
his irregular heartbeat.
Outside, the District Line
trains were less frequent;
even after they'd stopped
he felt there was always
another one coming –
like waiting
for the next hiccup.
The days at least had rhythm,
his first drink of tea
in the blue striped mug;
the walk to the shop
for the paper and back.
He turned again and searched
for the gap in the curtains,
slowly focused on the faint
glimmer of light and listened
for his next off-beat.

On the Rue des Tournelles

Night after night
in a Bar Tabac
a white rat still
on his right shoulder
he ordered cheese and wine,
the rat watching his moves
as he'd rip chunks to wipe
the remains of ripe Brie –
the rat's tail on his sleeve
like a well-rolled strip
of pink plasticine.

Two years later
I was to see him
on the steps of the Metro,
his stoop in the dark
more pronounced –
carrying gently
the space on his shoulder.

Between Stations

The man opposite today
had an air of decay that a dog-tooth
tie and a watch-chain
could not dispel.

He was drinking Lucozade.

Would he remember when
it had crinkly cellophane...?
(We smoothed it on measle-days
to save for the next eclipse.)

Sallowed and yellow
in the Piccadilly strip-lights.

When we stalled in a tunnel
between Holborn and Russell Square
he mouthed *Hell!* loudly and yawned.

East River Wind

In a Forty-Second Street theatre
scheduled for demolition,
she pounds the poet's dead words.

Later on the same block
the Italian padre exhorts
his diminished gathering

to bear witness this Christmas night
to the one who would be with them
all days, to the end

as crowds cross and uncross
themselves continuously
at each intersection.

The pretzel and soda vendor
on the corner of Fifth
breathes on his frozen nails.

The Fishing Hut

At the mouth of the river
the unused hut stood on.

At a time it was home
from home in the season
when he snatched a few hours
rising before dawn to slabs
of buttered bread and milk
in expectation of a full net.
Later he would sit in the doorway
mending broken creels
with a needle with an eye
bigger than that of a salmon.

When the cancer had taken his strength
dust settled on the cups
mould on the few blankets;
summers could come and go
and nothing would stir
behind the salt-stained window.

No Jitterbugging in the Aisles, Please!

We'd take them one by one,
chairs from emptied rooms,
to the park at our road's end.
We'd set them out in rows,
wait for the shuffling
guests who don't appear.

I'd put RESERVED
on the front two rows,
slip you last requests
while you'd hitch your too-slack suit,
ad lib a final solo
on that first silver sax again
till the shudder of the early
subway trains past the park
would signal day
and we'd head together,
your sax-case and my one
chair, to the station,
leaving behind flattened
grass, the scatter
of cloakroom tickets.

Foreseeing Death

i.m. Bill Heffernan

The prognosis was not good
you said as we listened
to coffee slowly working
its way through a filter
and I wanted to ask
if being a doctor
made news like this
easier or harder
to take in the end.

In the garden
you showed me
a spreading japonica
grown from a cutting
the previous summer
and spoke
for the first time
of those sorties by night
and the daily reckoning
for the rest of your life.

At the service I learned
you had ditched in the Channel
flying back from a mission
– only survivor out of twenty;
you were found the next day
close to death.

You'd never mentioned the plate
on your spine, or the medal.

Postscript

All of human life
is here he would say
reading Chekhov aloud
on a day in December
breaking perhaps to look
at the glittering frost
and the dead garden
as the postman rattles
the three o'clock silence
with the last few cards
for Christmas Eve.

Former Selves

After that she shifted the mirrors to a locked room,
lost the compact, no longer fixed
her hair, lipstick. She bought clothes
mail-order, avoided reflective
office-blocks, soon learned the new routes
losing sight in time of how she'd seemed.

Mirror images of the past misted over.

She watched as her mother grew old
and pondered the little distance
between them. She recalled her grandmother
dying in her sleep, the doctor
holding a pocket-mirror to her lips.

Holy Trinity Church, Clapham

January 6, 1994

I frame its classic columns
on this Epiphany feast,
keen to hold, to still
the fast-setting day:
from the Common's Southside
a funeral inches nearer
in a clear insistent drizzle,
the dipped lights witching,
quickening the dark.

A detached mourner in a black
two-piece –skin ashen –
advances stiff, unsoundly,
from the other side:
I watch her hold down
her brimmed hat with one hand,
proffer trembling
sympathy with the other.

Friday

It was a summer-wet city evening in the patio-garden; leaves were glossy with rain in the last of a reddened light. She liked to watch him in shadow, sitting to one side of the open french doors; she liked the way he held a beer, the way he packed his pipe, pressing down firmly with his forefinger, just like her uncle used to do. Should she tell him now, or later, or not at all. *We must cut back the firethorn*, he said, a voice startling the silence. She fingered the silkiness of her yellow dress, worn tonight for the first time. She had moved her lips to speak when the phone rang, rang again, rang insistently. Their eyes met for just an instant as she rose from her chair and moved towards the voice in the next room.

Home

In the dream I'm in a
white house by the bay

watching a funeral pass;
a woman in black chiffon

sits high in the second car.
I cry out, she stares ahead.

I drop the silent telephone
and shuffle through dead letters

in the hall: reading the names
I open the outer door

to the sound of lake water
and walk among ornamental trees

on an island adrift
in a tranquil sea.

RMS "Titanic"

My grandfather was lucky
and he wasn't lucky.

Bound for the Bronx on an
unsinkable sailing from Belfast

he jumped ship at Southampton,
went back to marry the girl he'd left.

She died at thirty-four,
four years before him.

If he hadn't gone back
she'd have married, anyway, maybe.

If he hadn't jumped ship
he'd have finished the trip on a sea-bed.

If *he* hadn't listened to his heart,
she'd still have died.

My grandfather was lucky
and then again he wasn't.

No Far Shore

It will be winter when I untie
the boat for the last time:
when I double-lock the back door
on an empty house,
go barefoot through bramble
and briar, measure each
stone step to the slip.

It will be night-time when I row
to the horizon,
steady in North-Star light
the darkened house at my back.

It will be winter when I draw
each oar from the water,
shiver,
and bite the cold from my lip.

II

Exile
is living where there is no house whatever
in which we were ever children

Lourdes Casals
(translated from the Spanish by Elizabeth Macklin)

The Orchard

My only grandmother had waist-long hair
tight in a bun in the daytime, wore black
for the husband and son she'd lost. Brown
hessian covered her piano. She never
mended the tied-up swing in the orchard.

But her bantam's eggs had whin-coloured yolks
and she griddled farls in the afternoon
to the tune of *Mrs. Dale's Diary* as I'd listen
and watch her floured hands from the window-seat.
Fasting from midnight and smelling of *Pears'*,
we'd take the Volkswagen to early Mass.
In the gas-mantle-hiss of evening, to a tall
clock's tick and the occasional hum
of a motor on the nearby Ballymena line,
I'd read the book she bought for my holiday
thinking I'd never heard of a sadder
thing than the scarecrow that longed to be liked.

I never saw my grandmother's piano
without its cover, never got to play
in the orchard.

Midday Bus

A lean man in a homburg
steps off the midday bus,
a cardboard Santa filled with chocolates
under his folded mac;
newly widowed and ill himself,
it will be a last gift
for his daughter at Christmas;
she never sees him again.

In later years the Santa
stands on the bakelite wireless
out-of-season, his sack
filled with medals and coins,
and her children play with the treasure
on a fading oilcloth. The day
we give him two coats of scarlet
my mother won't answer as I say
*It's not the same when he doesn't
bring you presents any more.*

Two Storeys

I

In a long, low house without stairs,
I lacked a skylight
to look out high on the town;
I wanted for stairwells, banisters,
where ballet-teachers and stepmothers
shrieked, and hooded friends met
in Bunty stories; hankered after Jane Eyre's
attic corridors where an incarcerated woman
would pine; ached for a boxroom where
the ceiling sloped, far from
a humdrum ground-floor kitchen.

II

Always after I've booked
and found myself ringing back
to check if the room could possibly be
on the lowest available floor,
I wonder what finally did for
the obsession with staircases, landings:
was it Mrs. Danvers or the Creole woman
crazed on rooftiles, or was it
my father checking fourth-floor
boarding-house windows and exits,
uneasy the long first night
of a city holiday.
    Thereafter
he would book caravans, bungalows.

A Woman's Place

Each day that dawned
she let in reality with
the milk and watched
neighbours in headscarves

slip through the lane,
waved to her children
over a half-net when
they turned at the gate.

Summer and winter saw
her return to half-warm
sheets and a candlewick
spread where she listened out

for the revving of engines,
maybe the hum of a mower.
The kitchen clock struck
regular on the hour.

Breakfast things sat
in the stillness waiting.

Backyard

A bird with feathers of blue
Is waiting for you
Back in your own backyard.
                      Billie Holiday

They were picking tar with a stick
from their new plastic sandals
when they caught sight of it caught
in a flapping shirt on the clothesline
– bluer than any blue they knew.

OK, their mother said, there was room
on top of the old radiogram;
so next day she brought back from town
a cage with a mirror and bell
and a blue bumper packet of *Trill*.

Word wasn't long getting out:
when Mrs McNeill came from Cedar Avenue
to claim her missing Zoë
she brought them a green bird instead
to show them, she said, her gratitude.

The new green bird wasn't much interested
in those children; wasn't bothered
by any reflection in a mirror; didn't even
sing, it seemed, in the same key.
But there was still picking tar with a stick.

Catching Your Death

All I can see of it now
is the rain that soaks the hay
that keeps wringing collies out of doors
that gutters from broken spouts
that falls in sheets on the day of a circus.

A hint of damp woollens at early Mass;
the sharpness of Loxene'd wet hair
on drizzly school-mornings.

Dripping plastic macs, squelched ankle socks.
The endless racing of drops on window panes.
And the unsolved puzzle of why
when you could come home soaked to the skin
the only thing absolutely forbidden
on pain of *catching your death*
was to swim in the sea when it rained.

The Half-Light

He hadn't seen the dog
in the oncoming darkness;
hadn't known what was ahead
until the soft scud of death
brushed his nearside –
so slight he couldn't be sure.

We stayed in the car
as he tried to explain,
admit maybe he was at fault –
but the owner harangued him long
and late and we watched
remorse curdle slowly to anger.

In September on that ill-lit stretch
his own dog ran straight out.
Without a word to the driver
he gathered her up in his arms.
Long after dark we stood
watching him dig in silence.

Upturn

My father at the front window
on a drizzled July Sunday
following a speck of orange
snail's pace across the bay –
too small to be of any matter.

Never at his best on a Sunday
he would fidget from Mass to tea-time
jingling change in the pocket
of a dark blue suit, adjusting
the radiogram to Athlone.

He'd check again on and off.
Only when it was lost
to sight beyond the headland
did he knock on a neighbour's door.
They had the boat out in minutes.

And found the men in time
gripping an upturned hull.
Their arms and hands were numb
and would be for weeks –
the papers said next day.

Sundays went on the same,
my father restless, jingling,
keeping a watch on the open sea.

Midnight Mass

It happened during the final hymn
in the front row of the side chapel,
faces from years, years back,
come in from the cemetery, stood

to sing – *a veil of hope,*
the weary world rejoices...
the kind that, living,
would have huddled at the back
skipped communion to light up.

At the second verse *Down!*
On your knees! even the early
leavers stood back to watch
them genuflect and shuffle out
as the choir soared above:
Oh night!
       Oh night divine!

Cushendall, 1959

Looking back to that Sunday
after a day on the mountain
pulling and plaiting rushes

I see her in a rose-print frock
slicing lettuce and hard-boiled eggs
while we wait on the front lawn

in the breeze coming off the sea:
the starched frock rustling
like dried paper as she brushed

in and out from the scullery
and I catch even yet
a hint of her Blue Grass scent.

Newsflash

Friday is fried herring,
bread and butter for tea.
I am in the doorway waiting
to see her chop fish-heads
into a basin, then the swift
clean cut lengthwise;
the kitchen reeks of rawness.

A newsflash drifts down the hall:
the President has been shot.
The knife halts in her hand,
my father's foot on the step,
her mouth opens to speak...
The Saint Brigid's cross on the back
door sways. The once-green
rushes could snap at a touch.

Outboard

I

He can feel it in his bones.
Too early for weather like this.

The last time he'll row her
out from the slip.
Tug the engine into life.

He can't remember a better morning.
Zigzags of light on water.

The prow lifts and she's out into the bay.

He takes in the shoreline.
The sleeping village,
silent as a postcard.

The sheeting of bluebells
on Layde.

II

Weeks in a hospital bed.
Endless, airless, side ward days,
he took himself on this journey.

Traded antiseptic for the smell
of low tide. Eyes tight shut.

III

Yesterday his neighbour's daughter
was home for the end of term.

She'd been awkward for a moment.
But didn't ask.

IV

Now it's just him and the water.
And the thought of going back.

Another few weeks of the treatment.
They think.
And he'll be back on his feet.

He cuts the engine.
Takes his sandwich from a Sunblest wrapper.

Tomatoes have moistened the bread
to a soft sweetness.

He licks a dry salt powder
from his lips. Leans back.

Settles to watch a vapour trail.

He could drift the day away.
Tomorrow too.
The odd cloud gathering over the Mull.

He can feel it in his bones.
Too early for weather like this.

A stab of something like fear.
Miles of darkness below.
He'd not like to lose sight of land.

Hallstand

He would wear sandals with socks,
roll shirt sleeves
back beyond the elbow.

She wore crisp frocks,
blues and yellows; on the lapel
of her summer jacket, a silver
flower-basket brooch,
a gemstone for every bloom.

All summer on shore walks
I'd dawdle, lag behind,
collect limpets and whelks.
That year I was eleven,
changing schools: they'd talk
about my new uniform,
the price of convent shoes.

Odd evenings there'd be a quiet
heavy tone: silence as I'd catch up.

The rest of the summer froze
to a single family snapshot –
I'm standing by the hallstand
watching
as she leaves for hospital.

Each long evening,
bored on the slipway,
I'd tear the legs off crabs,
one by one, throw them back:
smash volleys on gable walls,
until the light would finally go.

The sandals stayed in the airing cupboard
all that summer. And the next.

III

*The days running into each other, but oh the
distance between*
                    Louis MacNeice

Story-Teller

He tried hard to hold her
in the grip of that winter
but could see she had shifted
too far from his grasp;
but still he tried
to reach out with his stories
and the promise
of a life, just a life.

Where there is Hope

He offered the kind that didn't come
in capsules, in a country
where winter bit hard.

Nothing moved in her limbo.

Some days he brought chestnuts
warm from the corner
and once a glass terrapin
from the Oxfam window.

In December it was a tree
and six red baubles.

On her birthday they travelled
to the coast and she smiled
in the cold
for the camera.

When April moved in
on a still city evening
life quickened inside her
as she waited on the platform
in a short blue coat
afraid that he'd missed her.

Afternoons

for Matthew

I

The day they hired a Viva
her swelling tummy strained
against the web of a seat-belt.

Cream Crackers and cheese for lunch
on a dried-out verge
then on to a Chalfont farm

where she lifted a days-old pup
that clung for life to the bump,
licked salt from her sunburnt arms.

Those unruffled days before the birth
of sleeplessness, bottles and spoons
were to stay with her as years passed.

II

Today I sort spoons and mugs
enough for a bedsit,
tomorrow he leaves at six.

In wall to wall quiet I tune
to "Sounds of the Sixties", see
other lazy afternoons ...

... coffee, sugar, I include a book
of stamps, tell him to write.

Birds, Martinstown

It was a feature of that July.
Small towns of them congregated
on aerials, telegraph wires –
humdrum lines on a beaten sky.

She took it for a sign,
not just the summer's failing
but of tension in the wires.
She woke each day in a sweat

as random numbers of magpies
swooped aimlessly into view –
her mother would have kept count,
however long, till they evened.

On the day the downpour eased
he caught her look at Happy Hour.
Each waited for the other to let go.
She remembered there was still August.

Feet First

for Ruth

From the time things took a downturn
she hung on in
from the parting of the waters
to the sun's going down.

You might say, treading water,
with only the odd sighting
of an ankle to hold on to ...

You'd think that one
so deeply engaged
as to spend an age
in will-I-won't-I trepidation
would later exercise
due caution, always dipping
a toe in tepid waters first.

But since she made the crossing
she takes life on the wing
with feet that hardly
touch the ground; her head
stuck fast amid a crowd of stars.

Naming

When he first heard how we had named you,
your granduncle gripped a small hand
too tight and nodded:
Ruth among alien corn.

Only now, hearing another Ruth
– her young husband lately dead –
brush aside her name's destiny,
do I ask what burden we gave you
that spring day when green shoots
lightened the harrowed earth.

Leavetaking

The last thing he did
before leaving
at the first sign of light
was to fasten his watch
firmly on her wrist:
she woke slowly
into his morning,
kept pace with his days.

Matins

A churchbell cuts in.
Sunday: I wake alone.

From another continent
you call after touchdown:
our words tightrope –
rebound on the line.
All night I pictured you
eastward, cutting
a trail through stars.

I'm sending you the view
from our window: unchanging
dry branches, a hesitating
of squirrels... Can you see?
And can you catch that early
light that you know in my eyes
from mornings when we talk?

Waking

4:29 blinks:
beneath the bedroom window
first spits of rain glisten
the length of patio-greyness.
First-light strains in the blur.

Could be that dawn in Tosi
after a power failure in the valley
when we'd passed the night storytelling.

After we met I'd wished
on a shooting star high over
Eglantine Avenue. *Where?*
That's a helicopter searchlight –
it's up there every night now!
But it was too late:
the gods had already heard.

4:30 bleeps its arrival,
rain beats the window.

Moonbeam

Car- o-lin-a- Moon, keep shi- ning,
my father sang at the wheel
on Sunday summer jaunts.
Squeezing eyes tight I'd see
a silvered ballroom ball
in a satiny night-sky.

The smiling man-in-moon
I'd gouache'd for a daughter
mildews, hanging, in a cellar...
a daughter who, now grown,
no longer needs that
someone to watch over her
in black night-skies.

The Heart's Needle

I lie here with the late
night stations, listening for
my daughter's clicketing shoes
on the front path. I trawl
the airwaves, catch
a familiar strain... *summer's
gone and all the flowers...*

Yesterday she told me
leaving home frightens her,
then laughed at herself: admitted
to lying in the small hours
calculating what she'd need
– lamp, candles, Indian rug –
for her to have not left at all.

An engine slows in the street
below, then gathers speed.
No click. No key. Not yet.

Interior

Charleston Farmhouse, Sussex

Last burst of Indian summer
seeps from the pastel-wet orchard;
we find these rooms chill in the shade.

I take in the gentian sky,
red chimneys, a samphire on ridge tiles
from the library's half-open window.

For a trace of a second your fingertip
sparks with the silk of my blouse
and the afternoon misses a beat.

No longer do the thin wooden beds
under light-faded Omega prints
recall only the cold and the dead.

I discuss with the tour guide a gouache
of the church at Cassis, you flick
the pages of *À la Recherche* ...

Getting Ready

Saturday, late morning
off a crowded street:
in the L-shaped church
I read the names of martyrs,
stop at side altars.
The tabernacle is empty,
an ivory stillness, waiting.
In the courtyard
a bleeding *pietà*
blurs behind frosted glass.

An old woman in white trainers
arranges flowers for Sunday.
I remember to buy eggs
for my grown-up children.

Morning Shuttle

Pressure on take-off. You clench
in one fist the words: *Critical
most of the night.*

A sudden shift of light
floods the cabin, has you
suspended above clouds, clutching
at this early-morning's dream
of coffin-ships hulking
away from port, a plane
in Pittsburg that fell
like a shot bird. This is
limbo as long as it lasts.

Waiting for clearance
from the control tower,
latecomers stack
in the time-lapse above you.

Consultant

It's terminal – he says on the phone –
at her age – *not long.*
I wonder if he's sitting or standing.
At his end, another phone rings.

So this is how it's to be.
On five-o-clock mornings I see
the bedside waiting, the faces
at her funeral, milk in her fridge.

Misdiagnosis – he says on the phone –
not the sort of error
we like to make. He is sure
she'll be home in no time.

When you've woken each day for a week
to a dying and then – *at her age*
she could live for years –
you can never get back to before.

On My Birthday

for Cahal

You played the piano
at breakfast this morning
but it was Daddy's
voice I heard singing
beautiful dreamer
out on the sea ...

And you gave me flowers
for the middle years –
too many for one room.

The Quiet

They took breakfast by the tree
that Christmas Eve
the sharpness of dry pine
taking her back

to a room brimful of echo,
a room lightly lit
with the whiteness
of a Northern winter

where the after-scent of peat ash
edged the morning air: a sea-wind
wuthered the gable end
squalling, dying in the chimney

dying ... when he drew her back
to their room, to this present
the keenness of pure coffee
a new Christmas, a quiet start.

Gift

Like any *Songs of Praise* Sunday –
the toasting fork and one bar,
against damped, unleavened greyness.

This paling afternoon
a blackbird quivers, rattles
foliage against my window:
neighbourhood tablelamps
seep into November.

Sunday is expected to continue
throughout the evening
and well into the night
but I still hold yesterday's
white winter sunshine
caught at eye-level.
And the slow unwrapping
of a silk peacock scarf.

IV

Tonight I can write the saddest lines

Pablo Neruda

The Sea of Moyle

What brings me back here
year after year to this place?
I'd say it's the sea every time:
a sea that lapped, overflowing
in limpid starfish rockpools,
that erupted, seething, thrashing,
winter nights I couldn't sleep
and sometimes – on city evenings –
maybe waiting at the lights,
I hear the *hisssh* behind me,
the running of a tide.

First Nightmare of the Holiday

I rise and watch
from the picture window;
off the point a lighthouse
completes another vigil;
the flag on the fifth green
wavers in the breeze.
Nothing has changed
in all the years –
the dreams remain.

Nearing headlamps flicker on the high coast road.

The Heron

The sight of a heron
at the Salmon Port

on a December evening
was the first thing to bring

him back to a grip –
to a hold on life.

When his daughter
came for Christmas

they would walk together
at night on the rocks

and watch its outline
just visible in moonlight:

and when he wrote
at the kitchen table

the first Sunday in January
he told her

he was keeping-up the walks
but he'd not seen the heron

since the night she flew back.

Late Crossing

Past Carlisle
and a hundred dead
to the night boat
I chase vanishing
tail-lights through
relentless drizzle
and listen for news
of visibility in Malin.

Soon I will stand in
the teeth of a Gale Eight
on the *Ailsa's* deck
as morning berths
just out of reach
on an unseen coast
where a sole harbour lamp
signals an end to
the longest night.

New Year Departures

The parting was always a wrench:
standing to one side of the lane,
your worn brown V-neck pulled over
pyjamas for warmth; you'd shrug
and we'd wonder if this ...
if this was to be the last.

I'd reverse the lane's length,
pause on the corner – how small
you'd look in that moment, head high,
smile holding – a last glimpse, then
to Larne for the morning ferry:
conditions unfailingly bitter.

I'd picture you on every dip
and swell of those twenty-two sea-miles,
would see you in the kitchen ...
Would you watch the January bluster
from the back door, think only
of winds, high seas, stormy crossings?

November

You hated the days drawing in
putting an end to evening walking.
Instead you sat by the fire
looking older in your glasses
puzzling over the crossword
while your cigarette burnt down
to a long white ash.

May

It was not a month to die in;
you missed the warm June days
and long walks by the shore.
July was the cruellest;
I sat alone in the light
evenings waiting for your whistling
to break the stillness.

Last Things

I take your things
in a tagged plastic bag
across the resounding lino –
the car-keys and wallet,
your grey tweed jacket,
its smell of tobacco –
and pick up your car
from the empty park.
Don't choke, you'd say,
it should start first time,
your voice in my head
as clear as the ringing
of the evening Angelus.

Number Nine

In my father's house
you could hear the sea
in every room
see Scotland
on a clear day
from the garden.
The morning we buried him
there was a note in the hall
in his well-formed hand
BACK IN FIVE MINUTES.
No-one wound
the clock that night.

The new people
in my father's house
have sound-proof double-glazing
and windows in the roof
but I still see him
hunkering on the step
on a good day
with the first cigarette
or tuning in for
the late forecast
half-awake to the sound
of waves.

Tennessee Waltz

After his death she finds it –
top pocket of his suit –
the hotel-receipt kept
from his only daughter's wedding.

She puts it away in her box
high on the study shelf
still folded, creased, fragile

recalls the afternoon,
music, and how they led,
took the floor in a waltz

the one and only time
she'd danced with her father.

A House by the Sea

Each year she returns to the summer house,
listens for echoing waves.

In the paint-blistered porch she can see
a tangle of fishing-rods, sandals,
the dripping of swimsuits from deckchairs,
jam-jars of crabs and green slime.

Now only the geraniums are constant:
parched in a sun-dried clay
they watch from a warm front-sill.
Half-closing her eyes she's back
in the lap of a morning tide;
a seagull's call cuts the air,
light cries drift up from the shore.

She can even feel between cupped
and childish palms the beating
of a trapped, forgotten butterfly.

Barefoot, she relishes the grit
of sand on a midday verandah,
breathes the brackishness of wrack.

Coming Back

Last night you came to my door
nine years dead now
you looked no different:
*I need money for the taxi-man
his engine's still running.*

The eyes, maybe the eyes
were deeper – deeper set –
*Where have you been
all these years*, I asked:
*Oh just walking, walking the cliff-path,
looking for some place to settle.*

Woodsmoke

The thought comes to me today –
suppose I were to die
for an hour or two, rest
with you on Chapel Road:
in that chasm we'd breathe
September's woodsmoke, catch
the russet tang of apple.
We could listen to the river
rill over granite
then quicken for the open sea.
We wouldn't speak. No need.
Just to look on you again
and you to look on me.